D1588840

# IN THE HOUSEHOLD

## OF

## PERCY BYSSHE SHELLEY

University of Central Florida
Contemporary Poetry Series

# In the Household

## of

# Percy Bysshe Shelley

Poems by

Robert Cooperman

University Press of Florida

Gainesville / Tallahassee / Tampa / Boca Raton
Pensacola / Orlando / Miami / Jacksonville

Library of Congress Cataloging-in-Publication Data

Cooperman, Robert.
In the household of Percy Bysshe Shelley / Robert Cooperman.
p.    cm.—(University of Central Florida contemporary series)
ISBN 0-8130-1180-9 (alk. paper).—ISBN 0-8130-1181-7 (pbk.:
alk. paper)
    1. Shelley, Percy Bysshe, 1792–1822—Poetry.   I. Title.
    II. Series: Contemporary poetry series (Orlando, Fla.)
                    PS3553.O62915    1993
                821'.7—dc20            92-27087

The University Press of Florida is the scholarly publishing agency for
the State University System of Florida, comprised of Florida A & M
University, Florida Atlantic University, Florida International University,
Florida State University, University of Central Florida, University of
Florida, University of North Florida, University of South Florida, and
University of West Florida.


University Press of Florida
15 Northwest 15th Street
Gainesville, Florida 32611

This book is dedicated to my mother, Ann Fox, who read to me with the voice of an angel before I could read; and to my wife, Beth, whose love and encouragement have seen me through all of our good years together.

# CONTENTS

Tom Medwin Recalls His Cousin Percy Shelley
at Syon House Academy   1

Percy Bysshe Shelley Remembers Trying
To Raise the Devil While at Eton   3

Sir Timothy Shelley Lectures His Son, Percy,
Before the Latter Goes off to Oxford   5

The Reverend Jocelyn Walker, Fellow
of New College, Oxford, Explains the Expulsion
of Percy Bysshe Shelley   7

Lady Shelley Replies to Her Son's
Accusations of Adultery   9

Thomas Jefferson Hogg Rationalizes His Failed
Seduction of Harriet Westbrook Shelley   10

Thomas Jefferson Hogg on the Stage from Edinburgh
with Shelley and Harriet   12

Percy Bysshe Shelley Writes
to William Godwin from Dublin   14

John Philpot Curran Comments on Shelley's Pamphlet:
*An Address to the Irish People*   16

Miss Eliza Hitchener Leaves the Household
of Percy Bysshe Shelley   18

Percy Bysshe Shelley, After the Night Attack,
Tremadoc, Wales   19

The Honourable Robert Leeson Answers the Charges
of Percy Bysshe Shelley   21

Jack Tanner, After His Attack
on Shelley's House, Tremadoc   23

Thomas Love Peacock on Shelley's Decamping
for Switzerland with the Godwin Sisters   25

Percy Bysshe Shelley and the Godwin Sisters
Leave Lucerne for London  27

Captain Horatio Malone Sits with the Godwin Sisters,
Waiting To Be Paid by Shelley for
Ferrying Them to England  29

William Godwin Writes to a Friend,
Upon His Daughter Mary's Elopement
with Percy Bysshe Shelley  31

Mary Godwin Is Confined to Bed
During Her First Pregnancy  33

Claire Clairmont in the Household
of Percy Bysshe Shelley  35

Percy Bysshe Shelley After the Death
of His Grandfather  37

Harriet Westbrook Shelley on the Bank
of the Serpentine, November, 1816  39

Eliza Westbrook, After the Suicide of Her Sister,
Harriet Westbrook Shelley  41

Byron Comes to Terms with Shelley
Concerning Claire Clairmont  43

Claire Clairmont Accompanies Shelley
to the Execution of Seaman John Cashman,
After the Spa Fields Riots  45

Shelley Takes Leave of England Forever  47

Mary Shelley, the Night *Frankenstein* Was Born  48

A Military Gentleman Accosts Percy Bysshe Shelley
in the Rome Poste Restante  50

A Calabrian Priest Shares a Coach with
Percy Bysshe Shelley and a Lombard Merchant  52

Mary Shelley, Upon the Death of
Her Daughter Clara  54

Percy Bysshe Shelley, After the Death
of His Daughter Clara  56

Charles MacFarlane Remembers Accompanying the Shelleys
to the Etruscan Ruins at Paestum 58

Percy Bysshe Shelley, at the Ruins
of the Baths of Caracalla 60

Claire Clairmont Attends Mary Shelley
After the Death of Her Son William 62

Sophia Stacey Is Escorted Through
the Uffizi Gallery by Shelley 64

Henry Reveley, Mechanical Engineer,
Sponsored by Shelley 66

Tom Medwin Attempts Animal Magnetism To Alleviate
Shelley's Nephritis 68

Percy Bysshe Shelley Considers His Father-in-Law
William Godwin's Demands for More Money 70

Mary Shelley at San Giuliano, 1820 72

Mary Shelley at a Performance by Tomasso Sgnicci: Pisa 74

Shelley Goes Practice Shooting with Byron 75

Mary Shelley Learns of Her Husband's Illegitimate
Child by Their Maid Elise 77

From England, Leigh Hunt Writes to Shelley in Italy 79

Percy Bysshe Shelley Desires To Sail to the Near East 81

Claire Clairmont Celebrates Shelley's 29th Birthday:
Livorno, 3 August 1821 82

Shelley, Upon the Pirated Publication of *Queen Mab*, 1821 83

Percy Bysshe Shelley Is Shown by Lord Byron the
Fifth Canto of *Don Juan*: Ravenna, 1821 84

From Italy, Shelley Writes to Peacock About
the Cato Street Affair 85

Lord Byron Refuses Claire Clairmont Custody
of Their Illegitimate Daughter 87

Claire Clairmont, After the Death by Typhus
of Her Daughter Allegra at the Convent Bagnacavallo 89

Shelley Sees Spirits: Casa Magni,
Bay of Spezia, June, 1822   91

Captain Lorenzo Pola, After His Offer of Aid Was Refused
by Shelley, Aboard the *Don Juan*, 8 July 1822   93

Percy Bysshe Shelley Aboard the *Don Juan*, 8 July 1822   95

Captain Edward Trelawny at the Cremation
of Shelley's Remains   97

Lord Byron—After Shelley Drowns—Remembers
Their Sailing on Lake Geneva   98

Mary Shelley Receives Her Dead Husband's Heart
from Captain Trelawny   100

Edward Trelawny, After Mary Shelley Denies Him Permission
To Write a Biography of Her Late Husband   102

# ACKNOWLEDGMENTS

The following poems, some in altered form, have appeared or are forthcoming in the journals listed below:

*The Bellingham Review*: "Thomas Jefferson Hogg Rationalizes His Failed Seduction of Harriet Westbrook Shelley"

*Calliope*: "Miss Eliza Hitchener Leaves the Household of Percy Bysshe Shelley"

*Calypso*: "A Calabrian Priest Shares a Coach with Percy Bysshe Shelley and a Lombard Merchant"

*Coal City Review*: "A Military Gentleman Accosts Shelley in the Rome Poste Restante"

*the eleventh Muse*: "Mary Shelley at San Giuliano, 1821"

*Hellas*: "The Reverend Jocelyn Walker, Fellow of New College, Oxford, Explains the Expulsion of Percy Bysshe Shelley," "Percy Bysshe Shelley Aboard the *Don Juan*, 8 July 1822"

*Minotaur*: "Charles MacFarlane Remembers Accompanying the Shelleys to the Etruscan Ruins at Paestum"

*New Laurel Review*: "William Godwin Writes to a Friend About His Daughter Mary's Elopement with Percy Bysshe Shelley"

*Nightsun*: "Shelley Goes Practice Shooting with Byron: Pisa, Autumn, 1821"

*Oxford Magazine*: "Percy Bysshe Shelley Considers His Father-in-Law William Godwin's Demands for More Money"

*Poem*: "Shelley Sees Spirits: Casa Magni, Bay of Spezia, June, 1822"

*Proof Rock*: "Edward Trelawny, After Mary Shelley Denies Him Permission To Write a Biography of Her Late Husband"

*The Right Brain Review*: "Mary Shelley Learns of Her Husband's Illegitimate Child by Their Maid Elise"

*Roanoke Review*: "Thomas Jefferson Hogg on the Stage from Edinburgh with Shelley and Harriet"

*The Signal*: "Sir Timothy Shelley Lectures His Son, Percy, Before the Latter Goes off to Oxford"

*Slant*: "Percy Bysshe Shelley and the Godwin Sisters Leave Lucerne for London"

*South Carolina Review*: "Mary Shelley the Night *Frankenstein* Was Born"

*South Coast Poetry Journal*: "Lady Shelley Replies to Her Son's Accusations of Adultery," "Percy Bysshe Shelley, After the Night Attack, Tremadoc, Wales," "The Honourable Robert Leeson Answers the Charges of Percy Bysshe Shelley," "Jack Tanner, After His Attack on Shelley's House, Tremadoc," "Percy Bysshe Shelley Is Shown by Lord Byron the Fifth Canto of *Don Juan*: Ravenna, 1821," "Mary Shelley Receives Her Dead Husband's Heart from Captain Trelawny," "Lord Byron— After Shelley Drowns—Remembers Their Sailing on Lake Geneva"

*Sundog*: "Mary Shelley at a Performance by Tomasso Sgnicci: Pisa"

*Whiskey Island Magazine*: "Claire Clairmont, After the Death by Typhus of Her Daughter Allegra at the Convent Bagnacavallo"

I would like to thank Eleanor Swanson, Hugh Ruppersburg, and Patty Watson for their thoughtful comments and sagacious recommendations about this manuscript.

BIBLIOGRAPHY

Holmes, Richard. *Shelley, the Pursuit*. (New York: E.P. Dutton & Co., Inc., 1974).

Shelley, Percy Bysshe. *Selected Poetry and Prose*. Ed. by Kenneth Neill Cameron. (New York: Holt, Rinehart and Winston, 1965).

Spark, Muriel. *Mary Shelley*. (New York: E.P. Dutton & Co., Inc., 1987).

# Tom Medwin Recalls
# His Cousin Percy Shelley
# at Syon House Academy

I'll never fathom why Uncle Timothy sent
an aristocratic gawk of a boy
with wrists thin as fern branches
to that den of London bear-cubs.
Within fifteen minutes another boy
had stolen his shoes and a book,
and when poor Percy lashed out with slaps,
a ring formed, taunting him to punch
like a man and get his nose tattooed.

More prison than school,
a place even I found stifling,
and could offer Percy no help
or the others would've ripped him
like wolves on a crippled lamb.
The walls were dark, unclimbable,
the front gate locked, topped by spears:
a fortress to keep out savage Picts
or keep in sullen Sepoys ready to mutiny.
The elm-tree bell clanged us to frigid baths;
to meals prisoners in Bonoparte's wars
would have pushed away as if poison;
to classes wardened by Dr. Greenlaw,
his slaps lifting boys into the air
like canaries in a gale,
his classroom so drafty
our skin rose bumpy as chilblained parrots.

Even now I shudder to remember.
What Percy felt I can't imagine—
no wonder he blew up the bell,

left in peace at last.
The caning made him walk
like a veteran of the Peninsula Wars.

# Percy Bysshe Shelley Remembers Trying To Raise the Devil While at Eton

What I would have done had He risen—
conjured by my hate and incantations—
I shudder even to think of.
I do remember holding a skull
as I ran through midnight fields
to the place He was said to abide,
hearing the grass whip behind me,
something immense and darker
than night following.

I prayed for the Black Lord to rise
and raze Eton, break the boys
who made my life a Hell—
the older ones who beat me daily,
the younger ones who shouted,
"Mad Shelley!" and ran,
the ones who stole my books,
tore my clothes and kicked me
all because I refused
to fag for Matthews—
make his bed, clean his room,
fetch him sweets and tobacco—
as other junior boys slaved for seniors.

When I returned to my room—
the Devil still safely underground,
that skull dripping with dew and my fear—
I cursed that no other boy shared my digs.
I might have beaten him in his sleep,

3

Satan pointing the most tender places:
even if I knew I'd never raise a hand
to a sleeping lad, the image of innocence.

# Sir Timothy Shelley Lectures His Son, Percy, Before the Latter Goes Off to Oxford

Whores you may keep by the hundred;
a young man's blood burns for an outlet
or his brains will melt like toasted cheese.
I am therefore prepared to pay for a bastard or two.
Only, I pray you, call it something else:
money for books, gambling debts,
flowers for a friend's funeral.
But if, by God, I hear of you marrying
below our station, I'll disinherit you.
Let your sisters weep
that you wander the Continent shoeless,
having to steal bread, and sleep in alleys
with your bride like stray curs,
you'll not disgrace us by a match
with some butcher's daughter.

And I pray, no talk or writing of Atheism.
In these times of war with a France gone wild
on revolution and that upstart Corsican,
enough to get you executed for treason.
Let your tutors see an eager-eyed scholar.
Enjoy yourself, learn to smoke cigars,
to know a good cognac with one sniff,
to see if a claret's been property decanted,
to learn how, when the time comes,
to beget sons so our family line
will not snap like so many others.

You're not a bad boy, merely a wild one,
and a word or two from a man who's seen the world
should set you towards the useful life

you'll lead as head of our family,
protector of your sisters and brother John,
whom, I need hardly remind you,
I'll make my heir in less time than it takes
for your electrical cells to explode—
if you go too far with the pranks
your mother has spent nights crying over.

# The Reverend Jocelyn Walker, Fellow of New College, Oxford, Explains the Expulsion of Percy Bysshe Shelley

We'll have no Whig Atheism here,
no heresy and treason scribbled
in our tutorials and bookstores,
no deistic nonsense of watchmaker Gods
or no Gods at all; no pretentious students
like Percy Shelley trying to raise
the devil with electrical devices
while he rants about liberty and free love,
and publishes pitiful verses
under the name of that attempted regicide,
Margaret Nicholson, late of Bedlam,
now buried and unmarked in the ground.

When we brought him up on charges
for publishing *The Necessity of Atheism*,
he claimed that since it appeared anonymously,
we could no more prove him the author
than that bestial Frenchman, Robespierre.
We expelled him immediately, for failing
to answer questions, which, as a gentleman,
he was bound to answer when put to him.

Otherwise, the young egoist had us—
stating, as he should have, that the arguments
spewed in that execration of intellect
were merely to prove that "disbelief"
can in no wise be taken as criminal,
as the burning of a church most surely would be.

Thank God, Christ made his knees quake,
his tongue disconnect from his brain,
or he'd still be haunting our halls,
burning carpets with experiments
that smelled more of hell than chemistry;
screaming if anyone brought up Christ and religion:
you'd think Satan were singed with holy water,
a monomaniac, most assuredly; quite harmless,
a lamb of God, his acquaintances insist,
on any other subject.

Let him bleat in his father's house,
or wander the Continent.
Students come and go
like fleas on a wolfhound.
We shall be here forever.

# Lady Shelley Replies to
# Her Son's Accusations of Adultery

With Graham the music master?
Surely a boy of your imagination,
your egalitarian pretensions,
could find me a more fitting paramour.
Why not Hodge the gardener,
Smythe the Welsh stable-boy,
since this egg of yours was hatched in Wales,
from gazing at valleys and writing letters
to a schoolmistress plain as cabbage,
whose head you turned while plotting marriage
to this Harriet Westbrook, offensive,
but at least not the spawn of smugglers.

I believe your poor father is right;
you're mad—imagining not merely my trysts
with Mr. Graham, but that I'd sanction a match
between him and Elizabeth, so he could steal
into my bedroom while your father lay beside me,
to arouse a woman who never found
the grasp of passion anything more
than hard grappling to make sons who'd live.

All this comes from too much freedom—
allowed the run of the house
as if already a member of Parliament;
you should have been made
to live on gruel, cold baths, in unheated rooms.
Sir Timothy should cane you, or have Hodge do it—
in your mind your more likely progenitor.

# Thomas Jefferson Hogg Rationalizes
# His Failed Seduction of
# Harriet Westbrook Shelley

She was always fluttering like a canary
whose feathers you want to feel silken
between your fingers.  With Shelley gone,
trying to raise money from relatives
hard-hearted as old mousers, Harriet
was lonely as a caged song-bird,
its master never coming back—
or so she feared, that his mother
would cajole him into an annulment,
her virginity ruined like a flight feather
by buckshot and thoughtless hunters.

I was doing her a favor, or wanted to:
to show her a world beyond Percy's ravings—
clever, charming lad that he could be,
a perpetual boy in his enthusiasms,
a gentleman's son who'd rather demand money
of uncles than dirty his hands with work.

She needed someone to treat her like a woman,
not a doll or toy you'd call by pet names.
She wanted a man to take her breath away,
sweep her off her feet and directly into bed,
pluck her clothes off and make her laugh
then groan, her cries echoing like the screams
of eagles in the clutch of the mating dive—
someone to keep her from thinking
so much of herself and her morbid lust
for seeing her face pale as death.

Why should Percy have all the fun of wedlock—

he the demon preacher of free love?
I was bored by my role as their chaperone,
we three young as nestlings,
our bodies made for the sweet couplings
of doves that know nothing of marriage
or vows beyond, "Quick, I die for you!"
But the silly parakeet shrieked
when I tried to kiss her, locked herself
into her room, half fainted like a canary
on a curtain rod, a cat waiting open-mawed
below, for vertigo to plummet her down.

# Thomas Jefferson Hogg on the Stage
# from Edinburgh with Shelley and Harriet

In the coach—Harriet more
a sixteen-year-old school girl
and less his wife—Bysshe saw himself
an Ancient Mariner, yet hardly nineteen.
All my former heat for her quite cooled
to see them both so tragic-faced
and all the world a castle portcullis
they could never force or sneak through.

The dove-days of their elopement to Edinburgh—
its crazed preachers and strange dialects,
its wild northern lights and hilly crags
and workmen wild to talk trade-unions and Atheism;
its nights of Shelley and I laughing at clerics
and listening to Harriet read novels aloud
in her clear, glassy voice—
all as far behind them as Eden closing
on the lashed backs of Adam and Eve.

When the coach stopped at Berwick,
he disappeared, Harriet a mother pheasant
watching a fox devour her nestlings
to see him vanish; I found him on the Walls,
embankments above the open sea,
waves the very music of Hell—
a mirror of poor Bysshe's soul—
having cut himself off from family, inheritance
with this misalliance to a lovely doll,
no fit match for Bysshe, who had talked himself—
and her—into this yoking of lamb to lion.

When I finally coaxed him back,
he looked a half-drowned galley slave.
Harriet wept softly into a handkerchief;
I tried to tell a joke but neither heard it:
Harriet a girl in need of a rudder,
and Bysshe unable to steer his own life
let alone pilot a girl who whispers to Death
if anyone frowns at her.

## Percy Bysshe Shelley Writes to William Godwin from Dublin

Imagine Dante plodding lower into Hell,
hearing the screams, but knowing that none
of these lost souls deserved
the pain that impaled them forever.
Imagine a boy of eight, starving, in rags,
clinging to his mother like a kitten
trying to suck from a dead cat's teat,
then being seized by bailiffs and offered
the choice of the lock-up or the army,
while I stood by, too horrour-struck to speak.
"A felon," the sergeant assured me
when I finally sputtered a protest.
Imagine a woman beaten by constables
for stealing a loaf for her children,
a bottle to keep her leaf-thin lungs
from cracking on a Dublin night
that descends in cold forever
onto the narrow, crooked streets
that double-back like a labyrinth
constructed not by Daedalus, but by a God
who laughs at the poor and powerless.

Imagine, dear Godwin, packs of men
who once proudly wore the green—
now cringing for government posts.
It rips my heart like a pikestaff
to see man after man turned
into a monkey grinding a hand organ
for the joy of English governors
and their ladies craving diversion,
their footmen eager to smash
any beggar-woman who pleads for a penny:

a girl of twenty, face older than Sarah's
when that goat, Jehovah, filled her
with miracle progeny in the fairy tale
gullible men still swear by.

Forget politics, I tell myself
a thousand times a day, merely post
on every door a description of the sufferings
men so gladly turn a blind eye to—
as if the poor were nags for the knacker,
and not men and women deserving happiness.

# John Philpot Curran Comments on Shelley's Pamphlet: *An Address to the Irish People*

Typical of the English, to tell us
what's to our best advantage
before their feet sink into Irish peat.
Where was this witless calf of the gentry
when Wolfe Tone died in prison
by his own good hand
to keep a red-coat butcher
from tightening a noose around his neck?
And didn't I defend the United Irishmen
while this Bysshe was still slapping
his tutor's face with white fingers?
Judge Hardy did his best to condemn me
along with the others, but my voice sang
so greenly grand for Ireland and reason
even Hanging Hardy had to let us all go.

But now Percy Bysshe Shelley crosses
the Irish Sea in rough weather
and thinks himself an expert
on all things green and Catholic.
He dares berate me for selling out
my Irish birthright for a government post!
Let him spend years speaking, organizing,
watching his hair go grey before its time,
lines make gullies of his face
that was once open as a Galway meadow.
Let him talk himself blue before
a gauntlet of English magistrates
for the pardon of patriots,
each judge paid by the number of nooses
on John Bull's gallows.
Percy "Firebrand" Shelley? All palaver

at a harmless meeting for fancy women
and smartly-turned Dublin bucks
who laughed at an English monkey
with the gift of speech.

By God, I've earned my rest, my bit
of a government sop; it's tired I am
of haranguing all night and day
before judges who believe Ireland
but an English child that needs a cane laid
in great red streaks on its green spine.
Percy Shelley indeed! Why not Moses,
to lead us from our Catholic darkness!

# Miss Eliza Hitchener Leaves the Household of Percy Bysshe Shelley

He treats people like socks past darning;
now I'm the Brown Demon when once
he called me Wise Portia, his mind-mate—
before his Harriet's nervous tears
and her wolf-snouted sister's scowls
said I was no longer welcome.
They who begged me to leave teaching
as if a piece of meatless carrion,
to join them like Christ and his disciples.

To think I could listen to his gibberish;
that I loved his voice, his explosions
of what I took for a mind higher than mine;
that I adored our walks at Lynmouth
as if a maid mad with her first love;
that I let him take me behind the boulders
along the shore, the whole town watching,
as I sighed to be touched by great Percy Shelley,
who took no more notice of my gift
than he would of a servant bringing tea—
for all his pamphlets on the brotherhood of man.

A rich boy playing at poverty,
and I told him so when I took my leave;
and told him too I would have a hundred pounds
a year from him—compensation for losing my school,
my reputation among the folk at Hurstpierpoint.
I know he'll forget, his way with debts.
Still, it pleases me to get his pledge,
to let him know he's one of the privileged few
he hates—feeding off the rest of us.
So let him see his spots, the claws
he sharpens on mice like me.

# Percy Bysshe Shelley, After the Night Attack, Tremadoc, Wales

I accuse you, the Honourable Robert Leeson,
tyrant slave driver of the Tremadoc quarry,
grinder of the poor, the labourer;
petty aristocrat who'd have me imprisoned
for shooting a farmer's ewe trapped in brambles—
to feed a starving family of twelve;
you'd play the Judas who'd betray
his Christ's teachings to love the poor,
not starve them.  Any fool knows
no man can work with his belly whining
like a kitten in a sack, smelling the river.

From what divine edict do you,
the Honourable Robert Leeson, extract
the right to attempt murder,
to hire thugs to break my windows
and shoot at me, when I ran to defend
my pregnant wife, her shuddering sister
and my man-servant, an Irish peasant
who knows more of loyalty and honour
than you, the Honourable Robert Leeson?

How I wish you had the courage
of your hired killers:
I'd have left your loud, empty head
filled with one more hole.
I'd challenge you to a duel,
only one of your lackeys would shoot me
in the back—because I spoke out
for the Luddite weavers murdered
for their right of assembly and protest.
Why not render their bones into glue
and avoid the charge of squeamish hypocrisy?

No matter how well you keep the attack
from the local press, I know the truth
and so do you, Honourable Robert Leeson.
I spit on you and all your ancestors,
syphilitic whores and murderers.
I curse your descendants
unto the seventh generation
of your Jehovah's vengeance.
May you die screaming, seeing your bloody Christ
at the bottom of your canopied bed,
crooking his skeleton finger to the Pit
as he strips off his mask to reveal
my Lord Lucifer, King of the night's retribution.

# The Honourable Robert Leeson
## Answers the Charges of Percy Bysshe Shelley

I will tell you plainly and quietly and once:
I had nothing to do with that incident
at the house you were renting
but neglected to pay your landlord
any of the money you owed him.
I believe you made up this midnight attack
to be able to leave Tremadoc,
and, as always with men like you,
to smear a trail of bad debts
like snail slime until you can find
some fresh mud.

As for the smashed window, your being kicked,
the bullet hole ripping your nightgown—
easy enough to stage all that yourself
under stealth of darkness
with the help of your Irish understudy;
not the first time he'd have aided
one of your mad schemes
that try to turn the public order
into Satan's pandemonium,
but always end with your taking flight.

And as for an investigation
into the alleged foray
you so poetically describe?
I'll not waste the rate payers'
time or money on a man cut off
from his family like a gangrenous limb.
Take your low-born wife, her shrill sister
and the yapping accomplice
you talk to as an equal to avoid

giving the poor dog his bone of wages,
take your cracked seditions
and fly away, Percy Shelley.
In fact, we honest men of Wales insist:
may your master detain you below,
indefinitely.

# Jack Tanner, After His Attack on Shelley's House, Tremadoc

Jack Tanner knows to keep his mouth shut,
always has; but I'll say this—
if the Honourable had wanted
that braying ass dead, there wouldn't't've
been no smoking holes in his nightgown,
no smashed window, nothing of sound
nor fury, as the Bard says; just old Jack
mousing his way in while a door was unbolted
and biding his time in a dark corner
until dead of night; then slipping upstairs
and slitting that fool's throat, his wife
waking to more blood than's in a half-cooked
black pudding, his neck another mouth
she'd see smiling the rest of her life.

As it was, it took two smashed windows
before his young worship stumbled downstairs,
shrieking like that parrot the Honourable
bought off a gypsy that sailed the Seven Seas;
I had to take extra care to hit his nightgown,
to kick him only in his stomach, and not
smash his head in when he charged me,
screaming like a woman took by the fits.
I wanted to shut his trap for good,
—but the Honourable didn't fancy no inquiry
just enough force to scare little Percy off.

Worked like a charm, it did; vanished
in the morning, him and his pretty doll of a wife
with the hunted look in her eyes;
and her sister, what had a tongue on her
that could send the tide out at Hell's Mouth

without no thought of it ever returning;
and their Irishman of all work,
who had the look of a right smart lad
if he could be taught to keep his Dublin
rabbit trap of a mouth shut
and use his hands for something smarter
than nailing up leaflets
that get the quality all worked up,
so they can't sleep 'til they call Jack Tanner
and the honest service he provides.

# Thomas Love Peacock on Shelley's Decamping for Switzerland with the Godwin Sisters

What a blithe boy you are, Percy,
sobbing over French children
battling dogs for bones,
villages crumbled by fire and grape-shot,
fields gone to nettles from the tramp
of armies and spent shells,
corpses found in caved-in barns.

Your descriptions to your wife
eloquent to make a Mongol weep,
and in the next sentence of your letters
you ask her to join you, and bring
the articles of separation,
as would anyone touched
by the alchemy of your charm.

Were Harriet not in constant tears,
I'd spend my days reading your letters,
laughing like the lunatics in Bedlam.
Someone has to hold her when she sits
rock-rigid, a handkerchief suspended
in her white fist, her face paler
than if you'd slapped her
and said her whorish habits
had earned her a bed in the gutter.
She moans for hours,
asks how she has offended.
I turn away, torn
between tears and laughter
for the silly creature,

too china-fragile
to have married a panther like you.

My best to the Godwin sisters;
the rats that nibbled Jane's toes at Troyes—
to force her into your and Mary's bed—
must have seemed precocious brown cupids
to such a pretty butterfly as you.

# Percy Bysshe Shelley and the Godwin Sisters Leave Lucerne for London

London was dry as Arabia by comparison,
the landlord a brute, insinuating
that if we wished to barter Jane
reductions could be made in our rent.
Had she desired his pig-filthy hands on her,
I would have applauded her flaunting
the chattel laws of wedded whoredom,
but for him to degrade our heaven of love
made me rage higher than the flames
we kept up in the grates, our rooms
chilled like Matterhorn crevasses.

Two days we stood that hole;
rain like cannonade on the lead roof,
Mary and Jane she-cats spitting over a tom;
Mary never understood Jane needed soft talk
before bed when the horrours crept over her
like the rats that nibbled her fingers
in the auberge at Troyes, so vile a lair
a wonder the vermin themselves didn't decamp.

We took river buses to Rotterdam,
Mary ill, Jane reading *King Lear*;
the blinding of Gloucester sent her into such fits
Mary sat below with German ruffians.
Those diligences rocked like toy boats
London slum children float into maelstroms
of soaking gutters after a torrent.
At least we had the prospect of ruined castles
along the Rhine, mermaids in our minds
singing down from pinnacled shores, Mary joking
that Jane was Lorelei enough for a fleet.

At Rotterdam I coerced a captain
to ferry us to Gravesend on trust;
an east wind all but blew us overboard
and into my wife's drawing room.

After five hours of lies and pleading,
I persuaded her to pay that Channel pirate.
Before I return to her small-souled whining,
I'll walk barefoot the length of the Alps,
warmed by the cameo of Mary I carry in my heart.

# Captain Horatio Malone Sits with the Godwin Sisters, Waiting To Be Paid by Shelley for Ferrying Them to England

The younger one's a cheerful lass I'd chuck
under the chin if the other would stop
staring like a Pyrennes guard dog
when her eyes ain't licking the print
off a book whose title could blind a hawk.
But the little one spy-glasses my chest
as if she can detect the thick black fur
many a lorelei of the alley has fondled
before a blow or two against my typhoon.

Percy Shelley can take forever wheedling
my nine guineas from his wife.
Quite the young swell:  two pretties
waiting patient as dolphins for him to emerge
from the boudoir of his frantic mate,
willing to pay anything, I'd wager,
to have him between her decks again.

Nine guineas will fill my topsail,
and this pretty thing might shriek
and claim I misunderstood her cordiality.
If this Percy Shelley did run in the front
to escape out the back, I've had
almost payment enough
in admiring her dark eyes
and the way she swells her bodice.

If I could get her sister from this cab,
I'd show her what barter I can offer:
she the third wheel in Shelley's dog cart.

Such a mermaid I'd make of her:
the odour of salt air, the slap of surf
a more prodigious stimulant than ground antlers
lubbers use to purge their puniness

# William Godwin Writes to a Friend, Upon His Daughter Mary's Elopement with Percy Bysshe Shelley

He professes himself Plato to my Socrates,
then runs off with my daughter Mary, Jane as well,
who calls herself Claire in a fit of romance—
the sixteen-year-old confidante
to her step-sister and a poet so mad
I'd chain him in Bedlam for seducing my child
on the grave of her mother, lubricous ferrets
to defile the bones of my beloved Wollstonecraft.


This from a man who swears his wife's person
was offensive as a carcass to him.
She daily shows signs of a second confinement:
strange notion of disgust.
To think I opened my door, my mind, to him,
I allowed him to flatter me with loans
while creditors hunted him like hounds.


If he'd flush at Skinner Street again
I'd send a bullet through his devil's heart
before he'll grow weary of my daughter
and leave her with a brace of bastards,
Jane, too, embarrassed by family riches.


I'd spit on the pounds he doles,
but I'm reduced to playing the pimp.
Love of lucre one sty I've never groveled in,
but our household sputters on credit
and my reputation as a man of genius.

My wife hisses that my Mary has dragged
her silly kitten Jane-Claire into the gutter
and the least this Shelley can do
is pay for her trampled reputation.

# Mary Godwin Is Confined to Bed During Her First Pregnancy

"Best Mary," Percy calls me,
yet he tramps through London with Jane,
who now goes by Claire, mistress of romance.
Percy tells horrour stories by the evening fire
until she will sleep only in our bed,
nestled next to Percy like a kitten,
paws working for being weaned too early.

Who can blame him for seeking company,
my body a sack, ankles swollen,
this poor sputtering thing inside me likely
to drift still-born in the fetid birth-surge,
and Percy's wife already in possession
of a fat heir he will leave me for,
and take Claire—to terrify and pet.

Hogg calls when Percy and she are out.
I know Percy wants me to love him,
to show that I spit on the marriage contract
Percy reviles as worse than slavery.
Yet no matter how much I enjoy
Thomas's wicked speeches, his admiration,
I cannot descend to Horatio
when I've soared with Hamlet:
our coupling would be all the license
Percy needs to rut with Claire,
if he hasn't taken it already.

I'm nothing more than his mistress
even if he insists Harriet fills him
with vapours of the crypt.
Were she dead, he'd marry me;

and I'd condescend to Thomas, once.
I'd even take her children, love them
as if they had bulged my own stomach;
preferable to Jane or Claire, or Salome,
or whatever name she pounces on next.

# Claire Clairmont in the Household
## of Percy Bysshe Shelley

He wants me.
Only Mary's jealousy
keeps him from his desire.
I'd be one up on my step-sister:
she may have married Shelley,
but I'd have slept with both Percy
and that limping toad, Byron.

If not for me, those titans
of poetry may never have met.
When Mary wed Percy,
I had to throw myself at Byron or burst—
and he, club-foot cur,
condescended, once:
thrashed like a harpooned whale.

Each time he sees me
he hobbles away—
as if I were to blow him
a dose of the pox across the room.

He hates it that my mind
moves more swiftly than his,
that I best him in any argument,
that I lead his friend Trelawny on,
then drop the lying buccaneer,
telling him to send his master.

But if I can have Shelley,
I'll forgive even Byron.

Mary will get her precious Percy back;
I'm not greedy that way.
Nor will the act itself
please me overmuch.

# Percy Bysshe Shelley After the Death of His Grandfather

With that inheritance
I can return to the lodgings
where I left Mary,
can stop slipping from cheap hotel
to coffee house to back alley.
Not least, I can untie my wife
from my neck with an annuity.
Bless the old pirate,
even in his dotage twice the man
as my timid father. "Timothy,"
the perfect name for my progenitor,
genuflecting to very tyranny
of society and convention.

How suddenly miraculous London is,
a city bathed in sunshine;
delightful to tramp its streets,
to glance at shop windows,
stride into book stalls
and slap down shillings
from my own purse for a volume
that glitters with wisdom and beauty;
to walk freely with Mary,
genius honeying her lips,
her mind dazzling, gorgeous
as the Muses dancing on Parnassus.

I long to take her to Paris,
the literary salons will salute her,
applaud me for my discovery,

far greater than if Aphrodite
were found in a garret on the Left Bank,
tittering at the flattery
of tinsel Apollos.

# Harriet Westbrook Shelley on the Bank
## of the Serpentine, November, 1816

When they find my water-logged corpse,
Percy, may you die of shame,
may that whore sold to you by her father—
Godwin the Great—swell, and may her child chew
inside her like a mouse nibbling
a fat wheel of crumbly cheddar.

"You never understood my mind,"
you barked at me like a watchdog.
"We were mere friends," you said.
Friendship didn't stop you
from stinging me with your awful scorpion
to make a second child
bawling with your looks and sneer;
I left both children with my parents,
to disappear into these dark waters.

Were my Captain Walker not posted in the Bengal,
I'd not be abandoned at this beckoning stream,
his letters to me somehow lost;
or perhaps you've waylaid them,
the Devil, your master,
granting you the favor of their theft;
or perhaps he's dead, a tribal spear
quivering in his belly, my name
the last word on his lips.

Did you think I retired to a convent
when you sauntered off to the Continent
with Mary Godless and her step-sister in Satan?
You wrote me to join the three of you,
no mention of wife, only the separation papers
you wanted more than my body before we wed.

If hate could keep me alive, I'd be immortal;
but loathing, coupled with the voice
that whispers inside me to make an end,
is no sustenance for this tiny fruit
of my dear Captain Walker's love.
The world spins me giddy.
You'll smile to hear I'm pregnant with another.
"She was squeamish as only a true whore can be,"
you'll laugh. No one to slap your vulgar mouth
and challenge you to the duel you deserve
to die in, your mouse of the hour
wailing that her genius is murdered.

Water, black as dead leaves, rushes, hissing:
"Come, Harriet; it freezes but a moment."

# Eliza Westbrook, After the Suicide
## of Her Sister, Harriet Westbrook Shelley

You killed her, Percy Shelley,
as surely as if you had pushed her in
and held her below the surface
while she struggled just a little,
not unamenable to death, poor thing,
if your hand were performing the deed,
your latest cast-off and victim.

Now you demand custody
of the two children she bore;
your part, to thrust in seed and leave.
Where were you at Ianthe's birth,
when Harriet shrieked for ten hours
and I thought the poor struggling infant
would kick her apart?
Where have you been these last years
when Harriet was driven mad by loneliness
and the hounding of your creditors
while you thumped in goose down
or atop graves with Mary Godwin?

Call me an unpleasant meddler, or worse.
Still, you pick people up and drop them
like coats you expect your valet
to give away when they no longer please.
Harriet worshipped you, but you wanted her
lecherous as a baboon,
cunning as Catherine de Medici,
or else risk your eternal hatred.
She thrived on kisses and kind words,
withered when your scorn seared her
like Satan's rapier eyes.

May her tresses drag you to Hell,
and catapult her to Heaven,
your filthy soul the ransom
God desires in exchange.

# Byron Comes to Terms with Shelley
## Concerning Claire Clairmont

Suddenly, I'm the villain:
for jilting a woman whose only desire
is to bring into the world the child
she forced me to bear upon her.
She acts at keeping herself from weeping;
she sighs, touches her stomach
like an absentminded baboon,
while Shelley negotiates the terms
and I want to tear out my hair
or kick Claire into Lake Geneva.
Her added buoyancy will keep her afloat
until a Swiss fisherman discovers her
tangling his nets like a talking carp;
he'll curse the day he glimpsed
her seaweed locks—almost the Medusa
of my mathematically maniacal wife.

"I'll raise the child on the Continent,"
I stood firm, "if Claire comes to term in England.
She can visit, but only as an aunt."
Shelley agreed to keep Claire.
Let him pay for the hunger that dulls
her eyes whenever she sees anything
from lace to a man, voracious
as a sow for pounds or a pizzle.

She grunted after me
all over London, France, Switzerland.
She could have had St. Paul himself
lapping like a dog before her shadow,
able to turn a hymn into a menu of lust
for her hero of the instant.

Let Shelley try to support her;
his heavy-browed Mary scowling
like the very Devil he'd like to raise
and converse with as if a cricket champion.
He owes me—for expunging the schoolboy remarks
he made in every hotel registry in the Alps:
"Atheist, Philanthropist, my destination Hell."
Fool, to think the Inferno near Mount Blanc.
He'll know soon enough it's anyplace
Claire Clairmont rests her black widow head.

# Claire Clairmont Accompanies Shelley
## to the Execution of Seaman John Cashman,
### After the Spa Fields Riots

The magistrates needed a scapegoat:
a sailor with tongue lewd as a mynah bird.
Mary, as usual, too ill to support the masses,
so I told Percy I'd attend with him
if he held my arm, and kissed me—I teased—
should the odour of shot become too heavy.

That seaman's performance rivaled Keane,
shouting, "Hurrah, me hearties in the cause,
drink a toast for me that's to jig for you!"
When the pastor tried to pray,
Cashman told him to dance on air.
He refused the hood, and yelled,
"Give three cheers, you buggers, when I trip,"
and hopped on the trap.
I dug my head into Percy's shoulder.

"Murder!" he screamed with the rest:
rough working men, fists like wagon wheels,
caps dirty, truncheons stuck into belts.
"Take me away," I whispered to his white ear,
but he stood shouting, raising a fist;
then all fell as silent as dangling Cashman,
the only sound, the creaking rope,
his sailor's linen flapping in sudden wind.
Had darkness miracled the earth,
Percy might have fallen to his knees
a believer for once in his life.
But the breeze died, militia ringed us.

We crept away like field mice,
our genteel dress our passport—
to a good fire and hot tea,
and Percy pacing the tale
to Mary on her sofa, a finger
at the page she left off reading,
a look of worship for his bravery,
quite forgetting poor Cashman,
not even seeing insignificant me.

# Shelley Takes Leave of England Forever

Mary gripped my arm, to be buffeted
by white-capped waves, each a Mount Blanc.
One breath of that salt surge
and all the shackles of England fell away;
I was Prometheus released from bondage.

The children slept below, lambs
no March storm would dare harm—
while Mary, Claire, and I rolled
with the packet, its sails the Tricolor
atop the stormed Bastille.

A colonel's wife shivered near us,
reciting the Lord's prayer as wave
upon wave charged the deck.
Each time she groaned at the rail
she ordered her servant to repeat the litany:
as if a mumbled prayer could save her,
not a thought for her petrified companion.

"Behold the courage Christ gives his minions!"
I spat at the hypocrite
spilling unholy bile into the sea.
Mary and Claire pulled me away,
the silly woman too choked by vomit to hear me.

We strolled across the deck;
I was first to spy Calais
between curtains of rain,
my opthalmia falling away
like prig-Paul's blindness,
to reveal a heavenly continent;
Italy's arms wide as the love
a mother should give her oldest son.

# Mary Shelley, the Night
## *Frankenstein* Was Born

Percy, Byron and Dr. Polidori
talked of the spark that starts life,
joked of robbing graves for limbs and organs.
Byron recited some lines from Coleridge:
naked, deformed Geraldine bewitching Christabel.
Percy's eyes bored, horrour-red, through my bodice
as if a nest of asps were poised to strike him.
When Byron reached, "shield sweet Christabel!"
Percy shrieked as if a pitchfork had stabbed him,
Claire swooned, Dr. Polidori tossed water
at Percy's face, led him from the room,
whispering as if to a stallion in a storm;
Lord Byron read; and it was left to me,
as always, to pet Claire from her faint.
Bosom throbbing, she asked Byron
if he felt a ghastly presence.
"Only of bad acting," he muttered,
never lifting eyes from his page.

Later, when Percy and I lay in bed,
he said he couldn't shake that vision:
wolf's eyes instead of nipples under my gown
causing his terrour to mount as at the scraping
of a murderer dragging an ax upstairs.
He shivered when I placed a petting hand
on his hair; I turned, tears etching
acid ravines down my cheeks and jaws.

Later, I dreamt, of a man possessed by making life.
When he sees his creation fluttering eyes open,
its deformity hits him with a mallet;
he flees, but the monster laughs inside his eyes.

I woke with a shudder, started writing,
paragraphs dancing as if a hand
from my sleep were guiding the quill.

# A Military Gentleman Accosts
# Percy Bysshe Shelley in the Rome
# Poste Restante

When I heard that impudent beast
of an Atheist ask for his post,
I knew society would never rest
until I fetched him such a slap
as he'd feel in his grave.
So I strode up to the cur,
head no higher than my shoulders,
and knocked him to his knees.
Up the horrid homunculus sprang.
Again my palm struck his soft face,
again he collapsed,
Satanic parody of worshipful prayer
as he swayed, forced himself erect—
more ape than man—treachery itself
to trip me with his cane
then dive atop, foaming, snarling,
until I threw him aside
and kicked the rabid mongrel.

By God, I should have used
his blaspheming face for a football,
but let him off with a thrust in the ribs;
and still he climbed to his feet,
blood worming his mouth.
I had his cane now, and was prepared
to smash out his few remaining wits,
but a carbinieri ordered me off,
when that depraved pagan
should be beaten throughout Europe.

More dangerous than a thousand Huns,
a million dirty little Froggies,
these strutting Romans,
and every Hindi Thugee—
who can't help being heathen swine.
But damn-me, he was an Englishman,
and betrayed us all!

# A Calabrian Priest Shares a Coach with Percy Bysshe Shelley and a Lombard Merchant

The little English poet laughed at my terrour
of highwaymen, their muskets longer
than a Roman legionnaire's sword,
more ruthless than Hannibal and his elephants.
He snorted when I crossed myself
and fingered my rosary and crucifix.

To ease my mind, he said,
he drew out his pistols, useless
even for dueling, with his white hands.
The merchant also scoffed at my fears,
teased me with tales of round priests
found with their heads severed clean
as a guillotine's perfect slice; justice,
he claimed, "for the Church's merciless tithing."
May the hooks of Hell drag him down
to the Lake of Pitch by his ankles.

Meanwhile, Señor Shelley sat
with the face of a would-be assassin
and his pistol pop-guns
should highwaymen erupt like Vesuvius
from the Pontine Marshes' gloom.

We arrived in Naples in time
to witness a killing—
a ragged boy trying to rob a jeweler
was stabbed in the neck as he ran.
My Englishman quivered, almost soiled

his cravat with the bit of bread and cheese
I forced him to eat at journey's start,
the wine he had mincingly sipped
as if contaminated by rats
and not the generous gift of my Bishop.

"Take aim and fire, Señor Shelley!"
I laughed at his pallid face.
"But steady your hands first,
and offer a prayer to the Christ
you mocked, Who kept us from harm,
and turned our attackers into that rogue,
quite dead and harmless."

# Mary Shelley, Upon the Death of Her Daughter Clara

"Come!" Percy crooked a finger,
bidding us leave our safe, cool perch
in the Appenines for swampy Padua,
to have us near Byron and to suit Claire,
who hovers like a bat near her daughter,
the spawn of a single night with Byron.
He keeps the child from her
for fear she'll turn the pallid thing
into a shrieking wax-print of herself.

My twenty-first birthday was spent
packing and nursing Clara,
weak from the first fevers of dysentery;
while Percy teased Claire with ghost stories
and talked politics and poetry with Byron
and basked in the sun and wine of George's hospitality.

When at last we arrived by black gondola,
Clara's fever raged like starving curs
at a palazzo's trash heap.
She died before a doctor could lay a palm
on her forehead and declare her case grave.
Two days of grief and my husband
is off again with Byron.

Oh Percy, you sneer when he buys
girls from their parents,
but fail to see your thoughtless killing
of an angel: you cared more for Claire's comfort
than for the life of your own child.

In the dark of my room, Clara's ghost whimpers,
slaps away my reaching hands,
whines for her father
and the games he played with her,
before she had to leave his laughter.

# Percy Bysshe Shelley, After the Death of His Daughter Clara

Mary goes along in a dream
on the excursions I plan
with the care of military campaigns:
to keep our minds from dwelling
on our little, lost Clara
and not, as Mary surmises,
out of my natural callousness.

Goaded by Byron's hospitality,
I summoned my wife and daughter
from their mountain rest
to the hot plain of Padua,
never thinking my child too ill
for the journey.
Was I such a domestic monster
that Mary could not have written
to say Clara was too ill to travel?

I compounded the damage
by sending them further,
to accompany Claire to a Venetian physician—
Byron and I now inhabiting
one of his Lido palazzos—
fever raging, all unbeknownst to me,
in Clara's tiny body
like armies of soldier ants.

How many times I tried
to hold Mary's hand and apologize,
to bid her shake a little life
into her numb heart that shrinks
from me as if from a vampire?

But I can't leap the chasm
between us alone, can only offer
Pomepeii, Vesuvius, Virgil's tomb—
our outings always end
with cities in ruins, dead poets.

I long for England, laugh,
having tried to escape
that island of tepid hypocrites.
How can I tell Mary
that in my grief, I sought
the kisses of our maid,
who, even to Mary's dazed eyes,
grows heavy with my child?

# Charles MacFarlane Remembers
## Accompanying the Shelleys to the
## Etruscan Ruins at Paestum

Bless me if I recall a single column,
statue or stone temple from the ruins.
All I remember is Shelley driving
our team as if Tam O'Shanter whipping
his mare to escape all the witches of Ayr.
He made those black horses foam white
as the steeds of the sea;
a blush of the rose on his frail cheeks
that must have felt more sorrow
than a bachelor such as myself can imagine.

His wife wore mourning for their daughter.
She sat well back in her seat,
her face saying she was prepared to die.
Lucky woman, to be married to such a genius.

We rested at a collapsed bridge,
walked and plucked violets
large as hundred pound notes.
When we finally reached the temples
he lectured on their structural wonders,
but it all slips from my mind.
I see only his excitement,
Mrs. Shelley wandering the ruins
like a maid in a ghost story of fatal love,
the flowers we had given her
nowhere to be found in the carriage.

On the way back he tossed whole pockets
of *scudi* at beggars and ragged children.

"At least they're free," he shouted
above the clattering hooves.
"Not like those waifs you see
in England, worked to death by masters
blinded by venison and red wine,
careless as bears of the cubs they eat."

It was then Mrs. Shelley gave a cry
and drew even further back in the coach.
Shelley glanced at me; for an instant
I thought I had said something tactless.

# Percy Bysshe Shelley, at the Ruins
## of the Baths of Caracalla

From the Forum's arches
of Titus and Constantine—
emblems of empire that crumbled
into weathered sculptings—
I ramble to the baths of Caracalla:
smashed staircases,
vines thick as pythons,
walls overgrown with myrtle:
flower of love, of death.

A fitting place to compose
a poem of Prometheus.
Here, tyranny swaggered
naked and sweating:
fratricidal Caracalla,
killed by his own guards,
his blood rusting
the curative waters.
Here, I'm free
of our terrible winter—
Clara's death dragging Mary
into the rubble of grief.

In this flower-clotted ruin
the heart of Rome's in my hands:
monkeys jabber mockeries of orations
senators were forced to make
in praise of their demon-caesars.

If only Mary would join me here,
to rekindle our first days,
our bodies melting in sacred joy,

minds goading each other higher,
thoughts climbing faster than gibbons
can swing in their jungle liberty
from limb to creaking limb.

# Claire Clairmont Attends
# Mary Shelley After the Death
# of her Son, William

Mary, for once, doesn't scowl
when I enter a room.
Indeed, she leans on me
as an old woman hangs
on the arm of a paid companion.
Had I a shilling for the hours
I've listened to her tears,
I could purchase
Byron's affections for a month.

I mustn't joke:
bad enough that Clara died
and Mary blamed my selfishness
in a silence so black
it blinded me for a time;
but now darling William,
so soon after his sister.

I take what amusement I can—
sleeping till the sun descends
from this iron-hot summer sky;
teasing Henry Reveley,
a beau so backward, I fear
it's Percy he desires:
but he twitches like a mouse
before a cat's stalking shadow
even to entertain that possibility.

He's anxious as a child
patting a lamb's muzzle

while my face longs for a caress
in all this death plaguing our house:
Clara, Wilmouse, my Allegra
removed by Byron's cruelty.

I sleep, damp Mary's forehead,
listen to her and cluck sermons
about the flower budding inside her.
And when Henry proposed,
on bended knee pillow-propped—
his shaking hand soddening mine—
I laughed like a lark,
dawn drying its flight feathers.

# Sophia Stacey Is Escorted Through the Uffizi Gallery by Shelley

He charmed my chaperone into walking with Claire,
my small hand on his arm as we stopped
before pieces of statuary he thought essential.
Two moved him especially:
one—Niobe trying to shield her last child
from Apollo's arrows—
brought cascades of tears to both our eyes
when he told me of the Peterloo Massacre
and a pauper woman protecting her daughter
from the clubs of militiamen.
I gripped his arm more tightly
when he murmured like water dripping in a catacomb
of the deaths of his children,
bright William the latest.
Immediately, he shook himself—
a hunting dog flinging surf from its coat.
I longed to hold his gentle head
and offer the solace of a solemn kiss.

With another shake, he steered me to a Venus,
stooping as if issuing from her bath.
He laughed when he pointed to the joy
that danced on her lips and bare bosom
that he declared the softest marble in the world,
and confessed with another laugh
he had been often tempted to caress those stone doves.
He grew more red than I, then white,
his eyes, stars; my heart a mouse,
the warmth of an unnamable liqueur melted my legs,
but Percy caught my waist and sat me down,
my head resting on his dear shoulder—
until I heard Miss Parry-Jones

ask a guard in her dog-trot Italian
if he had seen a young English lady
with a gentleman "imprudent to lose
his scarf in this wretched weather."
She swooped down while Percy paced with Claire,
her head tossed back at some small joke,
her claws sunk into his arm,
when he glanced, all solicitude, at me.

# Henry Reveley, Mechanical Engineer,
## Sponsored by Shelley

His was a house cast into blackest sorrow:
two children dead in less than a year,
his wife unable to move for grief,
and when she did winch herself up
for a walk around her garden
or to my mother's house in Livorno,
she trailed a darkness more profound
than the mourning-streamers
breezes tormented behind her veil.

She barely noticed her husband,
so I never expected her to bid me
even good-day, good-evening.
Shelley listened, the gleam of a patron
in his eyes, while I explained my blueprints
for an ocean-going steamship
to ply the lanes from Livorno to Marseilles,
a vessel a hundred times more reliable
than his sailing boats, toys at the mercy
of every swell and swoon of doldrums and gales.

A thrill of Franklin's kite shot
through my arm when we shook agreement.
I could have embraced him,
would have tried to joke Mrs. Shelley
from her despair, but one look at her
and I felt myself a monster for exulting
in the face of a grief to drown Leviathan.

Claire tells me Shelley stays away from his wife,
unable to face her sobbing, her brute numbness.

I was about to tell her of her husband's
generosity in my own affairs,
but two tears crawled down her face,
mockeries of an infant's locomotion.
I left hastily, seen to the door by Claire,
who smudged a kiss on my lips:
this after she had laughed off my proposal—
following a month of wooing on her part.

Plans for boilers danced like gazelles
as I skipped back to Mother's villa,
wind in the dry September leaves
the chugging power of indomitable engines.

# Tom Medwin Attempts Animal Magnetism
## To Alleviate Shelley's Nephritis

I know I'm a clumsy beggar;
it's in Mary's eyes each time
I open my mouth, and shouts crash out.
Still, I've learned a thing or two
knocking about the Bengal
in His Majesty's Dragoons:
watching fakirs lay hands
on a forehead to draw the evil out
like worms from oozing ground.
I tried my skill
on the Colonel's daughter
when megrims gripped her skull
like a vulture's talons.
I earned a dance and more,
a Sikh servant pretending blindness.

So when Percy writhed from the shards
of nephritis gouging his side,
I stared him in the eye and whispered
as you would to a skittish colt
you know will make a champion;
I told him to hear nothing
but my cool, dream-inducing voice,
to feel only solacing fingers.
By God, he slept like a well-fed leopard,
no more pain thunderbolting his eyes.

Later, Mary carped he walked in his sleep.
"Percy will fall out the window,"
she wrung hen-thin fingers.
"But he won't," I smiled.

Her look told me she wouldn't mind
if I wandered the upper galleries
on rain-slick midnights
with all the windows thrown open.

# Percy Bysshe Shelley Considers
# His Father-in-Law William Godwin's
# Demands for More Money

Mont Blanc, if dropped into the Atlantic,
would sink from sight before you'd be appeased
of your hunger for my pounds.
On what do you spend the hundreds I send you
regular as the Bank of England
without whisper of interest or repayment?
Do you gamble? Whore? Toss purses to beggars?
Fall into the maws of speculators
like schools of shrimp swallowed by whales?

I give you half my annual income,
and still you demand to bleed me
because your daughter escaped
your tyranny in my company.
If not for Mary, I'd cut you off
like a dissolute son.

I shall tear my hair out
at the bills you amass more quickly
than Britain's national debt.
And now the crowning insult—
after our son William died,
you write to my wife, *your own daughter*,
that the child's death was deserved:
vengeance for her adultery with me,
her lawful, loving husband.

Practice, if not a little kindness,
at least some prudence to your daughter.
Consider the golden goose,

and how this gander
is cunning as a fox,
savage as a wolf
in protecting his own.

# Mary Shelley at San Giuliano, 1820

Percy's silences started honourably,
hiding Father's horrid letters
that accused me of adultery,
of murdering Percy's first wife,
saying God's vengeance was satisfied
in taking my babies;
then demanding that I pilot
Percy's wallet into his pockets—
entirely rat-gnawed by mad schemes
and my step-mother's avarice.

Now, Percy whispers to Claire—
plans to survey the political chaos
in England, he claimed, when I asked.
Even his gift for self-justification
withered like the last leaves
before my silent eyes.

I know he plots escape to Greece,
alone or with laughing Claire.
I know what they were to each other
on that trip to Venice—
a vain attempt to secure
her daughter from Byron.

I begin to understand Percy's first wife,
sweating on the Serpentine's banks,
taking the tiniest step forward
into cold, wet forgetfulness.

Barely an hour when Claire and I
are not spitting like tail-tied cats,

Percy enjoying the spectacle.
He'll hardly remember me
six months after they stand
giggling above my grave.

# Mary Shelley at a Performance
# by Tomasso Sgnicci: Pisa

Percy envies his spontaneous genius,
his gift for juggling words and action
without the clumsy crutch of quills
my husband and I must shuffle around on.
I could watch his ibex-agile gestures
for eternity, his eyes expressive
as Edmund Keane's in *Othello*;
yet Sgnicci goes the actor one better:
inventing dialogue as he treads the boards.

It's a vile lie Lord Byron spreads,
claiming Tomasso a sodomite.
Percy looks far more feminine-selfish
than the mastery that shimmers
from Tomasso's shoulders and hands,
his voice a fountain thundering epics
and tragedies—a Homer without
the marring defect of blindness—
a man Penelope might have fainted for.

Could I write fast enough, I'd copy
every word while the Muse
pets his black hair, strokes
his shoulders—his constant companion.
Far lighter work than fair-copying
Percy's hymn to Emilia Viviani—
casting her as his sun, while I dawdle
as the waning moon—frigid,
because he grasps me with ice tongs,
having forgotten, no longer caring
what makes me melt and flow.

# Shelley Goes Practice Shooting with Byron

I've received nothing but kindness from him:
the unlimited use of his carriage,
palazzos for me and my household.
So why do I wish to place
a load of lead between his eyes?
To still his voice booming wagers
as if I were a prince of his oriental wealth,
yet too proud to back down
from the assertions pounds make.

Our servants set up the bottles,
and I match him in shattering glass;
then we put tiny, hand-made targets
on the lower branches of trees;
and splatter them, Mary cheering me,
La Guiccioli a tempest of clapping hands
when Byron, scowling at her exuberance,
makes the bull's-eyes disappear—
a magician snapping his fingers—
sulphurous smoke all that remains,
and always he bests me by one or two.

It's the same when we talk all night;
I listen, nod, offer commentary
on the encyclopedic tale of his amours,
La Guiccioli asleep in their chamber above,
the salon still redolent of the garlic
she cannot get through a meal without.

The same, too, when he shows me unfinished poems:
I wish to rip them into wedding confetti,
but the world would be poorer for my spite.

Once, he showed me the first draft
of his "The Deformed Transformed."
I smiled, at last able to tell him
how feeble one of his productions was.
He laughed at the heart-shot,
sent the pages into the lit grate,
and thanked me for my searing frankness.
It was later I found out he possessed
another version, fair-copied,
and had it published to applause
in an England that runs from my poems
as if avoiding a belled leper.

# Mary Shelley Learns of Her Husband's Illegitimate Child by Their Maid Elise

You weary me, Percy;
once, my Prometheus,
now merely Jupiter of the boudoir:
Harriet, me, Claire, Emilia, Elise—
have I left any out?
The difference between you and Byron?
He paints no water colours of souls mingling,
while you sing to each new pair of ears
of soaring to heaven, until boredom
clatters you back to earth.
With each one, your worship sincere,
if brief.

This time there's a child,
palmed off as our coachman's,
a rogue you'll have to reckon with
even if you buy his silence.

Was it for heart-break
after our little Clara died,
the need to make new seed bloom,
no matter what ground it was dropped in?
Or because I turned from you,
when you grew tired of grieving?
Or had you finally wearied of Claire,
who tunes her nerves high as a violin?

Elise will abandon this child
faster than you chiseled free
of the Carrara grief in my heart.
Go carouse with Byron, cavort with whomever;

I'm cold as my mother's grave,
where I toppled for your blazing eyes,
your poet's tongue; my thighs blood-dark,
my stomach hammering guilt
I was too giddy to hear.

# From England, Leigh Hunt Writes to Shelley in Italy

My Dear Friend,
we live in dark, dangerous times—
when a man can be scooped up
as if by condors and picked apart
merely for his thoughts, let alone
for anything he commits to foolscap.
I tremble even as my quill scratches,
expecting a bailiff with warrant and club.

Now, I pray you, is not the time
for such incendiary stuff
as your *Mask of Anarchy*;
leave it in a drawer
and perhaps rethink what you've penned
in the heat of the heart-crushing
massacre at Peterloo.

Were I to print it,
noble, just sentiment—
and a poetry of genius—
my press would be smashed,
my poor person flung into prison, again,
forgotten by the cowering world,
the swaggering masters who mean
to strangle us or make us kneel
and thank them for our crushed shins.

Were you in England, I might
proceed, with you to stand by me
when the knock on my door
echoed like Waterloo cannons.
But you're in sunny Italy,

free from the fist that grips Britain;
Carlisle imprisoned for blasphemous libel
when he was *present* at Peterloo,
saw troops beating women and children.

But I shrill too loudly.
My best to your beloved Mary.
If only we could visit
in the land of oranges and guitars,
our haggard English faces
would turn ruddy as plums
in all that carefree warmth.

# Percy Bysshe Shelley Desires To Sail
## to the Near East

Italy begins to stifle, as England did.
I long for open ocean, a soul-mate
such as Claire or Emilia, to read with
and play chess, to deny ourselves nothing
when love bids us remake the world
in kisses sweeter than the milk of Eden.

Mary has become a yoke, dragging me
through this only life we will ever know:
her chains lightest when we ran off to Switzerland.
I heard the lock snap shut when we married.
The shackles grow heavier with her jealousies,
each carping word another link of steel.

When our children died, she turned brittle
as unworkable slabs of desiccated clay.
She drags her days, and mine,
inflicting more pain than the gall stones
clawing me to thoughts of suicide.
I'd gladly turn my dueling pistols inward
if only to stop her complaints
whenever I mention another woman.

Oh, for a boat and Claire, or Emilia—
that bright angel entombed in a convent
until her parents sell her to a rich man.
I'd set her free, use her proper petticoats
for the sails of our skiff
while we dallied on the teak deck
dancing like Venus's shell on blissful winds,
the world open as it was to lustful Odysseus.

# Claire Clairmont Celebrates Shelley's
# 29th Birthday:  Livorno, 3 August 1821

Mary may banish me, but Percy
is still my knight in white plumes—
visiting me on his birthday,
when Mary wished to celebrate
by droning dirges for their dead children
until all joy would have leaked
from his heart to be guiltily alive.

He crept into my chamber
and so made sleep impossible.
In the morning we rowed the harbour,
breakfasted, sailed beyond the jetties,
waves no higher than the creases
in my sheets the night before.
We talked, as wind rippled the canvas,
of making for Greece, to show
Mary's courtier, Prince Mavrocordato,
how real freedom fighters battle.

He looked at me with such love
I thought my heart would fly away;
he stared with such sadness—
yoked to yet another unworthy wife
with whose soul he could no more merge
than with the pigs that grunt
on the muddy outskirts of Livorno.

We returned, to dine, sharing wine
from one goblet—Lancelot and Guinevere,
Paolo and Francesca—oh, two adulterers
sick of our secret navigations.

# Shelley, Upon the Pirated Publication
## of *Queen Mab*, 1821

How many times did I beg Ollier
to publish the poems by which I yet
hope to bring down tyranny,
only to meet a silence profound
as the absence of God?
But now, by miracle,
William Clark of Cheapside discovers
an old copy of *Queen Mab*
and brings it out for workingmen.
Bless him for the theft.

I should slip all my radical works
under his door, and forget Charles Ollier—
my official publisher,
though little I've gained
from the twitching coward—
timorous as a rabbit scenting
a fox beyond its patch of clover.

It shames me to disclaim publication;
worse, to see the Censorship Board
pounce on poor Clark with a pack's
unleashed savagery on a fawn.
In my letter to Ollier
I paraded outrage for the theft
and detriment to my reputation
that I care as little for—
among the hypocrites of England—
as an old jacket I'd torn
while tacking into the Aegean's glory.

# Percy Bysshe Shelley Is Shown by Lord Byron the Fifth Canto of *Don Juan*: Ravenna, 1821

From "When amatory poets sing their loves,"
to "You'll pardon to my muse a few short naps,"
I read with mouth open, heart on fire
with admiration, envy, despair—
that I could never come close to such soaring.

I had thoughts of burning everything
I'd ever written, wanted to heat my grate
with the doggerel my vanity
had once convinced me would be immortal.
I wanted to take a poker from Byron's hearth
and smash his skull and eat his brains—
some of his divinity burning in my blood.

Here was the first poet of our age:
Wordsworth, Coleridge pitiful by comparison,
even Keats's *Hyperion* a shattered pot
when placed beside this deity
which men should worship more clamorously
than the most perfect diamond
wedged in the belly of a Hindu demon.

I wept, shook his shocked hand,
told him here was a work worth dying for.
He tried to flick away my words
as if a friend's unearned praise.
"Praise!" I wanted to scream.
"Hate! Loathing! Groveling Adoration!
nothing so puny as praise."

# From Italy, Shelley Writes to Peacock About the Cato Street Affair

*"The . . . Affair was an assassination attempt
by . . . radicals on Lord Liverpool's cabinet. . . . in part,
motivated by revenge for . . . the Peterloo Massacre, at
which a number of poor women and workers, peacefully
demonstrating for democratic reforms, were killed by the
police and the army. The Affair was found out before any
murders could take place."*—Richard Holmes

They played into Liverpool's hands
flexing to choke every workingman in England,
with no more thought than his charwoman
for wringing out a mop on her knees:
where he'd have her, forever.
The more the rulers send spurs into mobs,
the harder those shabby souls will fling
well-shod captains from their fine mounts,
and then what angels of anarchy
you'll have in Merry Olde England!

Is Liverpool so blind he can't see reform's
inevitable as yearly rings on a poplar?
Is he so used to drinking workers' blood
he eats the poor by reflex now?

He never will admit the masses of Eastcheap
are the same species as he and his cabinet.
So men will ever set matches to plots
that will detonate in their own faces,
worse, succeed in their murders—
to be crushed under artillery volleys
fired to wipe out a single fox's den.

I see it so clearly,
images fly at me as if to a gypsy witch
or a prophet Jehovah of Wrath filled
with agonizing epiphanies to speak out.
My Jeremiads will go unheeded,
incunabula for future hands.

# Lord Byron Refuses Claire Clairmont
# Custody of Their Illegitimate Daughter

Call me a carnal monster,
threaten me with lawsuits
and your invasion of my palazzo,
hoping to spy me thigh-deep in virgins—
to blackmail my acquiescence.

Nothing will pry my Allegra away—
to be raised by a whore
living with the Atheist Shelleys.
Call me a hypocrite as well:
a man who buys twelve-year-old girls
from their parents has no right
to banter religious fine-points
with his mistress of a single evening.

You must be fecund as a toad—
conceiving after so little provocation
as I was able to muster, performing only
from the hope that once you had groaned
sufficiently to lard your vanity,
you would leave me in peace.

One week in the Shelley household
and some dread fever would grip
Allegra with skeleton fingers:
their lives a curse upon children—
killing two already, and Percy
all but shoving his first wife—
crammed with yet more spawn—
into the icy Serpentine.

I know to what measures
your hysteria will goad you—
and I swear to thwart them all,
even to throttling your throat
that has always run to fat.
Better to dance the gallows tarantella
than cede my daughter to your poison.

# Claire Clairmont, After the Death by Typhus of Her Daughter Allegra at the Convent Bagnacavallo

Mary and Percy advised resignation
when I wrote to them of snatching my daughter
from Byron's clutches:  more a Cenci
than the filicidal monster of Percy's verses.
I wander their wet rooms by the sea,
the Gulf of Spezia spills no less water
than the tears I've shed for Allegra.
The first floor of their huge
rented boathouse slimy with surging surf,
I thump my face against its walls.

George thought I wanted my poppet
only as a wedge back into his bed.
Like all men, a worshipper of his mirror,
saying I had dropped her like a brood mare
and could thus care nothing for her;
to him, I craved only the peerage
attached to George Gordon, Lord Byron.

Percy has the sense to stay away from me
while Mary and Jane Williams take turns
mopping my brows and talking
in tones of mourning doves.
If only I had forged the letter
in Byron's hand and gotten Allegra away
from the convent before contagion kissed her
with fetid breath—the same taste
as George's lips on the one night he filled me
with the life he insisted on killing.

I heard Percy mutter to Mary
that Byron will condescend
to my arranging the funeral:
"Better he should carve his coffin!"
I raved, and rushed to find Percy's pistols.
He and Mary held my arms, led me back to bed,
while I thrashed and roared,
threatened to murder the whole world.

# Shelley Sees Spirits: Casa Magni, Bay of Spezia, June, 1822

They began with Allegra, wandering
the sea-soaked terrace,
her hands twigs in December,
imploring me to save her
from Byron and Claire.
Waves lapped her tiny unshod feet,
soaked her death-dress, her tresses
wild as eels in a net.

Next, as I prepared for sleep,
I saw Edward and Jane in my doorway—
blood heavy as sea water
on their sopping hands; they shouted
waves were surging into the house.
He pointed to the higher ground
beyond the beach, impassable brush;
Jane's bosom heaved beneath cheesecloth,
her arms reached for me,
lips ripe as blood-filled roses.

I screamed, hoping to wake,
but I *was* awake,
and when the fleshly Jane and Edward
tried to calm me with promises
of tea, brandy and a dry bed,
I shook them off, paced the beach
like a vagabond, moon shattering
its million shards
onto the shimmering bay.

Last, worst, was watching myself
as I bent over Mary's bed
and took her throat in my hands,
my teeth grinding millstones,
her cries garbled as crows;
then silence, while I watched
the dream figure wipe his white hands
as if a butler drying silver.

I fainted; when Mary hovered
over me with salts, her face
a pietà of worry, I told her
it was the old nephritis in my side,
added that the pain had passed
and I could return to my bed.
I tottered to my chamber,
afraid to open my eyes all night.

# Captain Lorenzo Pola, After His Offer
# of Aid Was Refused by Shelley,
# Aboard the *Don Juan*, 8 July 1822

Crazy not to board my *felucca*
making for Livorno's safe harbour.
Waves flamed his schooner's decks
like lava from Vesuvius;
crazier still, he refused to take in sail,
wind tearing canvas like leaves and twigs.

I told him, "Reef your sails or you're lost!"
His friend tried to lower one,
but this Shelley, who thought himself immortal
and his English-built boat unsinkable,
flung the other's grip from the rigging.
With rain and surf pelting me
like stones to kill an adulteress,
I still could see the look
of murder on this Shelley's face.

His cabin-boy cringed,
the mast threatening to pull free
and fling him into the cold arms
of the wolf-howling waves.
Shelley ignored my plea
to allow the drenched mariner to come aboard,
the boy too frightened to move
without his English lord's consent.

What could I do but race
that devil-storm into port?
The bodies washed ashore ten days later,
picked over by fish, scraped by rocks and coral.

Saint Elmo grant them
a short term in Purgatory;
I think this Shelley wanted to die
and hadn't the stomach to face
that guillotine of water alone.

# Percy Bysshe Shelley Aboard the *Don Juan*, 8 July 1822

I've sailed in worse storms:
that voyage from Dover at least Force Ten,
and I manfully on deck with Claire and Mary,
singing sea shanties to defy Jehovah
to bang and smash.
This storm hasn't that bite,
no matter that my thoroughbred
can't carry the ballast
of that ox of a packet.

I could hurl curses at God
like Satan or Prometheus,
dare that old, bald bully
to pummel us with both fists,
then I'd laugh, having beaten
the toothless toad at his game
of threats and rage.

How she darts!  I feel alive
for the first time in years:
running like a monkey to keep
her sails from tearing,
to man the rudder
that fights me as I've wished
Mary would battle in bed,
when she lies like a virgin
resigned to the brute she blames
for our daughter's death.
Had I the time, I'd tear off
shirt and trousers, stand glorious
in the storm that Williams sobs
will fling us overboard.

"Have faith, man!" I shouted,
ripped his hand away that tried
to lower the sails.
"Let her run before the wind
like the great race-horse she is.
We'll hold on as she gallops
victorious into Livorno's harbour."

# Captain Edward Trelawny at the Cremation of Shelley's Remains

When the brains seethed like porridge
in poor Shelley's splintered pan,
Byron swam to his yacht.
A poet who uses a skull for a wine cup
should have more stomach in him.
Shelley wouldn't have run if Byron's body
were sliced away in the blue-sabered flames.

Hunt and I watched until only bones remained;
the beach facing Elba—its fortress that held Napoleon—
a fitting backdrop for our vigil.

Shelley once told me that poetry's
the dying ember of inspiration.
Here was proof:  the best of him
embers blown on a fair wind
to whatever heaven awaits poets
and amateur sailors with more courage
than sense to leave port
in a squalling sea.

When Byron deserted—a handkerchief
covering his mouth and nose—
he told me to save him the skull.
I swore he'd not possess
another wine stoup of such precious metal.
If he wanted a relic, I'd have gladly
guided his hands into the raging cremation.

# Lord Byron—after Shelley Drowns—
# Remembers Their Sailing on Lake Geneva

The simplest thing, had he asked,
to teach him to swim; any dog can master it,
so a gentleman should have taken to water
as greyhounds to coursing hares.
But despite our near swamping
off the rocks at St. Gingoux,
he never approached me for lessons.

When our rudder snapped
like a sabre thrust at a boulder,
and waves reared over the prow like stallions,
he sat calm as a Hindu expecting
his next incarnation to begin momentarily.
He took off his coat when I removed mine
and waited for either the squall to subside
like a sleeping brat after a tantrum,
or for it to kill him when we jumped in.

He preferred drowning to the humiliation
of my dragging him to the safety of shore
not a hundred yards from our rocking skiff—
if he struggled, a slap or two
to quiet him, as a she-wolf cuffs
her cubs to keep them near the den
when she hunts by night.

There were times afterwards,
when I could have jokingly pushed him
into gentle surf no higher than his knees
and shown him how to stroke, breathe, kick.
I never did, though he worshipped sailing:
too proud to ask,
I too indolent to volunteer my knowledge.

Still, he has the death he coveted,
more a hero than I'll ever be—
chained to Italy by my mistress
and her brother, who can't stop
confiding to his friends
that he dines nightly with Byron.

# Mary Shelley Receives Her Dead Husband's Heart from Captain Trelawny

Give me my husband,
not this lacquered box,
a charred organ I dare not look at
and retain what few wits I hold
more desperately than I did
my wandering Percy when he lived.

If only I could believe in the monster
I had my Frankenstein create—
I'd build my Shelley again,
starting with this heart.
Had the authorities not demanded cremation
when his ruined corpse washed ashore,
I could have forced life to imitate art,
bastard sister of hope.

Had he not taken that volume by Keats
he might have seen storm clouds
hunching like Spanish bulls;
had he a true sailor on board
with the barefoot tenacity of a squid,
he might have scudded to port
before death grabbed, shook them.

Protect me from poets who wander
with other women or over the waves;
make my son afraid of the deep water
that rode over Percy like chariot wheels;
make him hate Trelawny's pirate gallantry.

At least Percy's safe from Claire
and every other woman who smiled,
swooned to be talked to
by my self-exiled laureate
and Prophet of Hell.

# Edward Trelawny, After Mary Shelley Denies Him Permission To Write a Biography of Her Late Husband

She's turning an eagle into a canary
with her cult of the conventional,
as if anything was ordinary about Shelley.
She's afraid of what I'll find
in his letters, diaries,
the essays and poems he hadn't published;
afraid of the proof that he bedded Claire,
that he desired Harriet even after he ran off
with Mary—that there were a thousand women,
all throwing themselves at his feet,
whom he took in a succession so dazzling
a wonder he had energy for his second
lawfully wedded wife and the web of morality
she tried to spin round his heart.

Her *Frankenstein* a work of supreme drabness:
denying the only breathing being in the novel—
Victor's repugnance for his Adam
a mirror of Mary's horrour at the pain of pregnancy.
It wouldn't surprise me if Swiss blood
plodded her veins, the wife of a Titan.

His life deserves a narration
as only I'd tell it because I loved him,
seeing through to the truth beyond facts
that merely clutter.
What a life wants is the aura
that his had and that I could enhance.

God rot you, Mary Godwin Shelley,
sitting in your spider's weeds of widowhood,
telling the world what a dutiful husband,
what a loving father Shelley was
when the man can no longer defend himself.

# UNIVERSITY OF CENTRAL FLORIDA
# CONTEMPORARY POETRY SERIES

Diane Averill, *Branches Doubled Over with Fruit*
George Bogin, *In a Surf of Strangers*
Van K. Brock, *The Hard Essential Landscape*
Jean Burden, *Taking Light from Each Other*
Lynn Butler, *Planting the Voice*
Daryl Ngee Chinn, *Soft Parts of the Back*
Robert Cooperman, *In the Household of Percy Bysshe Shelley*
Rebecca McClanahan Devet, *Mother Tongue*
Rebecca McClanahan Devet, *Mrs. Houdini*
Gerald Duff, *Calling Collect*
Malcolm Glass, *Bone Love*
Barbara L. Greenberg, *The Never-Not Sonnets*
Susan Hartman, *Dumb Show*
Lola Haskins, *Forty-four Ambitions for the Piano*
Lola Haskins, *Planting the Children*
William Hathaway, *Looking into the Heart of Light*
Michael Hettich, *A Small Boat*
Roald Hoffmann, *Gaps and Verges*
Roald Hoffmann, *The Metamict State*
Greg Johnson, *Aid and Comfort*
Hannah Kahn, *Time, Wait*
Michael McFee, *Plain Air*
Richard Michelson, *Tap Dancing for the Relatives*
Judith Minty, *Dancing the Fault*
David Posner, *The Sandpipers*
Nicholas Rinaldi, *We Have Lost Our Fathers*
CarolAnn Russell, *The Red Envelope*
Robert Siegel, *In a Pig's Eye*
Edmund Skellings, *Face Value*
Edmund Skellings, *Heart Attacks*
Ron Smith, *Running Again in Hollywood Cemetery*
Katherine Soniat, *Cracking Eggs*
Don Stap, *Letter at the End of Winter*

Robert Cooperman is the author of *The Trial of Mary McCormick, Seeing the Elephant,* and numerous uncollected poems. He has taught at Bowling Green State University, the University of Georgia, and the University of Baltimore. He lives in Pikesville, Maryland.